TEN in the BED
And Other Counting Rhymes

Zita Newcome

WALKER BOOKS
AND SUBSIDIARIES
LONDON • BOSTON • SYDNEY • AUCKLAND

Yasmin

Charlie

Melissa

Jordan

Rosie

Yuji

Anna

Angelina

For Jane and John,
with love

Sam

First published 1999 by Walker Books Ltd
87 Vauxhall Walk, London SE11 5HJ

This edition published 2004

2 4 6 8 10 9 7 5 3 1

This collection and *One Step, Two Step* © 1999 Zita Newcome
Five Big Ice-creams © Claire Ross-Masson
Here Is the Beehive by Emily Poulson © J. Curwen & Sons Ltd
Reproduced by permission
The Three Bears © Hasbro International Inc. Reproduced by permission

This book has been typeset in Bembo

Printed in China

British Library Cataloguing in Publication Data:
a catalogue record for this book is available from the British Library

ISBN 1-84428-504-9

Contents

Baa, Baa, Black Sheep

Baa, baa, black sheep
Have you any wool?
Yes sir, yes sir, three bags full.
One for the master,
And one for the dame,
And one for the little boy
Who lives down the lane.

Moo, Moo, Brown Cow

Moo, moo, brown cow
Have you any milk?
Yes miss, three jugs smooth as silk.
One for you,
And one for me,
And one for the little cat
Who sits in the tree.

Chook, Chook

Chook, chook; chook-chook-chook,
Good morning, Mrs Hen.
How many chickens have you got?
Madam, I've got ten.
Four of them are yellow,
And four of them are brown,
And two of them are speckled red –
The nicest in the town!

The Three Bears

When Goldilocks went to the house of the bears
Oh, what did her blue eyes see?
A bowl that was huge,
A bowl that was small,
A bowl that was tiny, and that was all,
She counted them, one, two, three.

When Goldilocks went to the house of the bears
Oh, what did her blue eyes see?
A chair that was huge,
A chair that was small,
A chair that was tiny, and that was all,
She counted them, one, two, three.

6

When Goldilocks

went to the house
of the bears

Oh, what did her
blue eyes see?

A bowl that was
huge…

She counted them,
one, two, three.
(last verse)

They growled at
her, grr, grr, grr!

When Goldilocks went to the house of the bears
Oh, what did her blue eyes see?
A bed that was huge,
A bed that was small,
A bed that was tiny, and that was all,
She counted them, one, two, three.

When Goldilocks ran from the house of the bears
Oh, what did her blue eyes see?
A bear that was huge,
A bear that was small,
A bear that was tiny, and that was all,
They growled at her, grr, grr, grr!

Five Bananas

Five bananas on banana tree,
Three for you and two for me.
Five bananas on banana tree
Oh! I love those bananas!

Four bananas on banana tree,
Two for you and two for me.
Four bananas…

Three bananas on banana tree,
Two for you and one for me.
Three bananas…

Two bananas on banana tree,
One for you and one for me.
Two bananas…

One banana on banana tree,
Half for you and half for me.
One banana…

No bananas on banana tree,
None for you and none for me.
No bananas on banana tree
Oh! I love those bananas!

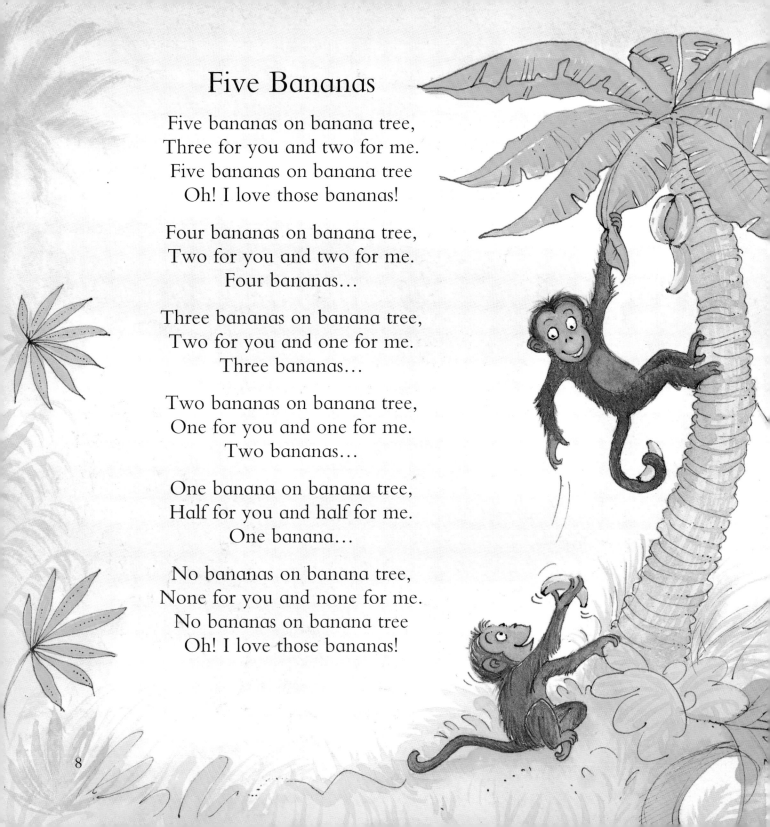

Three Elephants

One elephant went out to play
Upon a spider's web one day.
He thought it such a tremendous stunt
That he called for another little elephant.

Two elephants went out to play
Upon a spider's web one day.
They thought it such a tremendous stunt
That they called for another little elephant.

Three elephants went out to play
Upon a spider's web one day.
The web went CREAK, the web went CRACK
And all of a sudden they all ran back.

When I Was One

When I was one I ate a bun
The day I went to sea;
I jumped aboard a sailing ship
And the captain said to me:
"We're going this-way, that-way,
Forwards and backwards, over the deep blue sea.
A bottle of rum to fill my tum
And that's the life for me."

When I was two I buckled my shoe…

When I was three I hurt my knee…

When I was four I fell on the floor…

When I was five I learned to dive…

When I was one

I ate a bun…

I jumped aboard
a sailing ship

And the captain
said to me:

"We're going
this-way,

that-way,

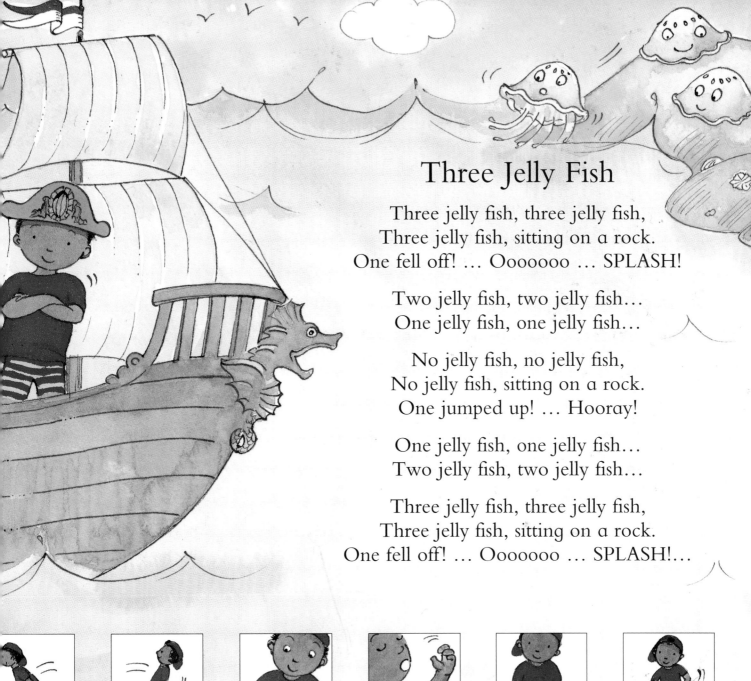

Three Jelly Fish

Three jelly fish, three jelly fish,
Three jelly fish, sitting on a rock.
One fell off! … Ooooooo … SPLASH!

Two jelly fish, two jelly fish…
One jelly fish, one jelly fish…

No jelly fish, no jelly fish,
No jelly fish, sitting on a rock.
One jumped up! … Hooray!

One jelly fish, one jelly fish…
Two jelly fish, two jelly fish…

Three jelly fish, three jelly fish,
Three jelly fish, sitting on a rock.
One fell off! … Ooooooo … SPLASH!…

wards

and backwards,

over the deep
blue sea.

A bottle of rum

to fill my tum

And that's the life
for me."

Hickory, Dickory, Dock

Hickory, dickory, dock,
The mouse ran up the clock.
The clock struck one,
The mouse ran down,
Hickory, dickory, dock.

Hickory, dickory, dock,
The mouse ran up the clock.
The clock struck two,
The mouse said, "Boo!"
Hickory, dickory, dock.

Hickory, dickory, dock,
The mouse ran up the clock.
The clock struck three,
The mouse said, "Whee!"
Hickory, dickory, dock.

Hickory, dickory, dock,
The mouse ran up the clock.
The clock struck four,
The mouse said, "No more!"
Hickory, dickory, dock.

Johnny Taps with One Hammer

Johnny taps with one hammer,
One hammer, one hammer,
Johnny taps with one hammer,
Then he taps with two.

Johnny taps with two hammers…
Then he taps with three.

Johnny taps with three hammers…
Then he taps with four.

Johnny taps with four hammers…
Then he taps with five.

Johnny taps with five hammers…
Then he stops.

Ten Fat Sausages

Ten fat sausages
sizzling in the pan…

One went POP!

and another went
BANG!…

Ten fat sausages sizzling in the pan,
Ten fat sausages sizzling in the pan.
One went POP! and another went BANG!
There were eight fat sausages sizzling in the pan.

Eight fat sausages sizzling in the pan,
Eight fat sausages sizzling in the pan.
One went POP! and another went BANG!
There were six fat sausages sizzling in the pan.

Six fat sausages sizzling in the pan…

Four fat sausages sizzling in the pan…

Two fat sausages sizzling in the pan,
Two fat sausages sizzling in the pan.
One went POP! and another went BANG!
There were no fat sausages sizzling in the pan.

14

Jumping Beans

One, two, three, four,
Beans came jumping through the door.
Five, six, seven, eight,
Jumping up on to my plate.

Five Cream Buns

Five cream buns in teddy's shop,
Teddy's shop, teddy's shop,
Five cream buns in teddy's shop
Round and fat with a cherry on top.
Along came *(insert your child's name)*
Hungry one day,
She bought a cream bun
And took it away.

Four cream buns in teddy's shop…
Three cream buns in teddy's shop…
Two cream buns in teddy's shop…

One cream bun in teddy's shop,
Teddy's shop, teddy's shop,
One cream bun in teddy's shop
Round and fat with a cherry on top.
Along came *(insert your child's name)*
Hungry one day,
She bought a cream bun
And took it away.

Five Big Ice-creams

Five big ice-creams
With sprinkles on the top.
Five big ice-creams
With sprinkles on the top.
And if teddy takes one
And gobbles it all up –
There'll be how many ice-creams
Standing in the shop?

Four big ice-creams…
Three big ice-creams…
Two big ice-creams…

One big ice-cream
With sprinkles on the top.
One big ice-cream
With sprinkles on the top.
And if teddy takes one
And gobbles it all up –
There'll be no big ice-creams
Standing in the shop.

The Animals Went in Two by Two

The animals went in two by two,
Hurrah! Hurrah!
The animals went in two by two,
Hurrah! Hurrah!
The animals went in two by two,
The elephant and the kangaroo.
And they all went into the ark,
For to get out of the rain.

The animals went in three by three,
Hurrah! Hurrah!
The animals went in three by three,
Hurrah! Hurrah!
The animals went in three by three,
The wasp, the ant and the bumble-bee.
And they all went into the ark,
For to get out of the rain.

The animals went in four by four…
The great hippopotamus stuck in the door…

The animals went in five by five…
They felt so happy to be alive…

The animals went in six by six…
They turned out the monkey because of his tricks…

The animals went in seven by seven…
The little pig thought he was going to heaven…

The animals went in eight by eight…
The slithery snake slid under the gate…

The animals went in nine by nine…
The rhino stood on the porcupine…

The animals went in ten by ten…
And Noah said, "Let's start again!"

Here Is the Beehive

Here is the beehive
But where are all the bees?
Hiding away where nobody sees.

Here they come creeping
Out of their hive,
One and two and three, four, five.

Two Little Dickie Birds

Two little dickie birds sitting on a wall,
One named Peter, one named Paul.
Fly away, Peter! Fly away, Paul!
Come back, Peter! Come back, Paul!

Five Little Froggies

Five little froggies sitting on a well,
One looked up and down he fell,
Froggies jumped high,
Froggies jumped low,
Four little froggies dancing to and fro.

Four little froggies sitting on a well…
Three little froggies sitting on a well…
Two little froggies sitting on a well…

One little froggy sitting on a well,
One looked up and down he fell,
Froggy jumped high,
Froggy jumped low,
No little froggies dancing to and fro.

Number One,
Touch Your Tongue

Number one, touch your tongue.

Number two, touch your shoe.

Number three, touch your knee.

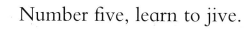

Number four, touch the floor.

Number five, learn to jive.

22

Number six, pick up sticks.

Number seven, point to heaven.

Number eight, open the gate.

Number nine, touch your spine.

Number ten, let's do it again!

Five Little Firemen

Five little firemen standing in a row;
One, two, three, four, five, they go.
Hop on the engine with a shout,
Quicker than a wink the fire is out!

Four little firemen standing in a row;
One, two, three, four, Whoosh! they go.
Hop on the engine with a shout,
Quicker than a wink the fire is out!

Three little firemen standing in a row;
One, two, three, Whoosh! Whoosh! they go...

Two little firemen standing in a row;
One, two, Whoosh! Whoosh! Whoosh! they go...

One little fireman standing in a row;
One, Whoosh! Whoosh! Whoosh!
Whoosh! he goes.
Hops on the engine with a shout,
Quicker than a wink the fire is out!

No little firemen standing in a row;
Whoosh! Whoosh! Whoosh!
Whoosh! Whoosh! they go.

Five fat peas in a peapod pressed,

One grew, two grew

and so did all the rest...

Until one day the pod went POP!

Five Fat Peas

Five fat peas in a peapod pressed,
One grew, two grew and so did all the rest.
They grew and grew and did not stop,
Until one day the pod went POP!

One Potato

One potato, two potato,
three potato, four,
Five potato, six potato,
seven potato, more.

Five Little Leaves

Five little leaves so bright and gay
Were dancing about on a tree one day.
The wind came blowing through the town,
Oooooo … oooooo.
One little leaf came tumbling down.

Four little leaves so bright and gay…
Three little leaves so bright and gay…
Two little leaves so bright and gay…

One little leaf so bright and gay
Was dancing about on a tree one day.
The wind came blowing through the town,
Oooooo … oooooo.
The last little leaf came tumbling down.

Ten in the Bed

There were ten in the bed
And the little one said,
"Roll over! Roll over!"
So they all rolled over
And one fell out,
And he gave a little scream
And he gave a little shout, "Yahoo!"
Please remember to tie a knot in your pyjamas,
Single beds are only made for
One, two, three, four, five, six, seven, eight −

There were nine in the bed…
Please remember to tie a knot in your pyjamas,
Single beds are only made for
One, two, three, four, five, six, seven –

There were eight in the bed…
There were seven in the bed…
There were six in the bed…
There were five in the bed…
There were four in the bed…
There were three in the bed…

There were two in the bed
And the little one said,
"Roll over! Roll over!"
So they both rolled over
And one fell out,
And he gave a little scream
And he gave a little shout, "Yahoo!"
Please remember to tie a knot in your pyjamas,
Single beds are only made for one.
Single beds are only made for one.

Two Fat Gentlemen

Two fat gentlemen met in a lane,
Bowed most politely,
Bowed once again.
How do you do,
How do you do,
And how do you do again?

Two thin ladies met in a lane…

Two tall policemen met in a lane…

Two small school boys met in a lane…

Two little babies met in a lane…

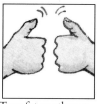
Two fat gentlemen…

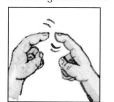
Two thin ladies…

Two tall policemen…

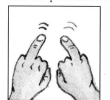
Two small school boys.

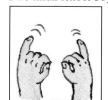
Two little babies…

One Man Went to Mow

One man went to mow,
Went to mow a meadow.
One man and his dog,
Went to mow a meadow.

Two men went to mow,
Went to mow a meadow.
Two men, one man and his dog,
Went to mow a meadow.

Three men went to mow…
(you can carry on until you get to ten)

One Step, Two Step

One step, two step, find my teddy bear,
Three step, four step, going up the stair.
Five step, six step, now start to hop,
Seven step, eight step, come to a stop!
Nine step, ten step, going very fast,
Eleven step, twelve step, how long can it last?
Thirteen, fourteen, going very slow,
Fifteen, sixteen, not so far to go.
Seventeen, eighteen, nearly at the chair,
Nineteen, twenty, have a rest with bear.